MUSINGS: THE JOY'S JOY

Tabatha J. Jones

Southern Women Publishing

Southern Women

To the Triune God and the he and she
That have encouraged the me;
Saw the greater that resides deep within me;
Who pushed and pulled for me
To be all that I am chosen to be.

CONTENTS

UN^{APOLOGETICALLY ME}

Before I formed you in the womb, I knew you. Before you were born, I sanctified you. I have appointed you a prophet to the nations.

JEREMIAH 1:8 (WEB)

HAVE YOU EVER?

Have you ever.....

Wanted to but didn't?
Should have but wouldn't?
Could have but thought not?
Would have but opted out?

Have you ever.....

Went to the door but not opened it?
Opened your mouth but kept quiet?
Drove up then just pulled off?
Desired hard but chose soft?

Have you ever.....

Loved but kept it to yourself?
Bought a book that never left the shelf?
Went to work but your mind was at home?
Been in a full room yet felt all alone?

Have you ever.....

Needed someone so much but your heart was closed?
Tried to hear but through your nose?
Reached to touch but couldn't move?
Really won but imagined you'd lose?

Have you ever.....

Lit a candle then just blew it out?
Felt sudden pain but then not shout?
Bought dinner then just threw it away?
Called a friend but had no words to say?

Have you ever.....

Picked a college yet not go?
Got the job but was a no-show?
Made the money then rammed up a hog's cast?
Came in first but waited and became last?

Have you ever.....

Grabbed the gun and not aimed?
Felt different but acted the same?
Chewed your food yet you did not swallow?
Smiled yet endured sorrow?

True, life is full of misery and strife
Yes or no
Come or go
Give or take
Sleep on or wake

True, the choice is yours
Lift your voice
Make your choice
Be the true
YOU!

ALWAYS BE CONCRETE

A-B-C is always as easy as 1-2-3
Truth is, it be just what it be
But in time or destiny, we all will soon see
Time isn't on cruise control for you nor for me
Although we act like this and that is for me
But not for we.

Boo, ALWAYS BE CONCRETE!

Get up off your do-not-a-thing
Stop opening your mouth with no-thing you sing
Do not pursue a man wearing another woman's ring
Be patient and your man will bring you your own bling, bling
So don't get mad when he takes his bling and his ring
And places them in another woman's sweet thing.

At the same time,
My brother, don't be so quick to wine and dine,
The next sister that lets you feel her mind,
As she blows your mind,
Searching brother after brother to find,
That one brother she can call "mine."

AAHHH, my dear, ALWAYS BE CONCRETE!

We beat the bush until it burns.
Work all day every day,
But still no money we've earned.
We grind the milk, until the butter-we've churned.
Read book after book, for knowledge we learn.
But see wisdom my darling,
One is given.
So, let love be your greatest concern.
Stand on truth, so the lie you discern.

But, hey babe, ALWAYS BE CONCRETE!

At the end of the day
Your do outweighs your say
So let your actions pave another's way

Gather your thoughts,
Get up on your feet,
Make a joyful noise,
As your hands meet,
Drive safely down these paved streets,
Carry yourself humbly and discrete,

Always, yes ALWAYS BE CONCRETE!

I AM LOVING ...... ME

I am loving me, officially.
The real me, some try not to see.
So what if you don't take the time to see me?
Still, I will love me, constantly.

For how can I be true to me,
When I've forgotten how to love me?
'Cause I've been trying so hard to love
He and she and it and thee,
That I've neglected the fact
That I can't love you
If I don't know how to love me.

I am loving me, officially.
The real me, some try not to see.
So what if you don't take the time to see me?
Still, I will love me, constantly.

You can say what you unofficially think of me.
You can even repeat what "they" say about me.
No matter, the true me will rise.....
High as the listening skies.
'Cause to me, I plan to always be me.
You might not like me,
But at the day's end,
I'm gonna, I gotta .... always be me
For without me, there is no.....
ME!

You going out, trying to be you should be easy.
It shouldn't bother me that you're being you.
It shouldn't bother you, by me being me.

I am loving me, officially.
The real me, some try not to see.
So what if you don't take the time to see me?
Still, I will love me, constantly.

We can get up everyday
And make the most of what everybody else's got.
But I double dare you to step out
And shoot your own shot:
Go back to school,
Be brave and jump,
There is no "I'm too old" rule.

I am loving me, officially.
The real me, some try not to see.
So what if you don't take the time to see me?
Still, I will love me, constantly.

Last time I checked,
"Our Father" said love is who He is.
Who is He?"
I'm glad you asked.
He is God.
It is He who sits high and looks low.
He is not a game.
He is not a show.
For God is love.

Wake up, get up,
There's no more sleeping in bed,
Or on your feet,
Or wherever your heart beats.
When it comes to being spiritually fed,
One tends to complain.
My brothers and sisters
Stop driving yourselves insane.
'Cause you don't know

What it means to love.....
What it really means to love.....
What does it really mean to love?

Some body's gonna miss the point
And say I'm trying to get you to love me.
The focus, the aim is for me to love me
And for you to love you, too.

I love me .....
I love me!
I L-O-V-E M-E!!
Do you love you?
God loves you and me!

If you don't love you,
But you say you love me,
Then something is wrong with you.
'Cause you can't love me
Unless you first know how to love you.

I am loving me, officially.
The real me, some try not to see.
So what if you don't take the time to see me?
Still, I will love me, constantly.

UNEASILY BROKEN (DEDICATED TO <u>WTKR</u>)

A man of God
Who works hard
Who is dedicated
And true to God.

He might be the youngest in the house
But by far is he the quietest mouse.
He sees what he wants and sets the goal,
The drive and desire renders him as an old soul.

You, too, like He
Envision more and more.
You, too, like He, will soon soar,
High above the average bar.
Sooner than later, you, too, will be a glorious star.

It's from the piano to the keyboard,
From the drums to the guitar,
From the vocals to the productions
And many, other things, thus far.

He's shining bright
Helping others get right,
His dreams are insight
Awaiting the right time to take flight.

Son, brother, father, minister, entrepreneur,
Encourager, friend, pastor, teacher,
Anointed, appointed, chosen and used
From Pop to Reggae, to Rhythm 'n Blues
To Gospel and Swing, Poetic and Jazz,
He's the Ace, the Trustee, and the Head of the class.

Ambitious, and busy
Committed and dedicated
Energetic and faithful
Glorious!

He's a major and a minor, a whole and a half
A scale and a chord, loud and soft
Lyrical and harmonious, pianissimo and forte
Right hand and left, bass and lead
OMG, what's left?...

It is all in the work you do
For you do well what you work to do.
Anointed hands, eyes, mind, all through
I declare, it is all in the work you do.

THE SINGLE, SAVED AND SATISFIED WOMAN (10/1999)

I looked, I searched, I attempted to find,
A good faithful man I could really call mine.
Someone to hold me to mold me, to really be there,
A special someone, our lives together, we would share,
The goods, the bads, the ups, the downs,
The no-matter-whats, he would always be around.

I wanted a lover of my heart, my mind, my body and my soul.
I wanted someone, together, our lives would unfold.
I wanted him to be a Christian and a friend, all in one.
I wanted He and I to be a total of one.

Along my search, most I found,
But never that true love,
He would possess an earthly love,
But not that love as He above.
He would be a lover of my body,
An attempted lover of my mind.
For he, the lover of me all
I did not find.

I looked, I searched, I attempted to find,
A hardworking man that I could truly call mine.
I found not my equal, but one who is greater,
I found, yes, my lover, my Lord and my Savior.

.

He told me He would save and then satisfy me.
I told Him I would truly trust Him.
He showed me He would never leave nor forsake me,
I told Him I would love and believe Him.

He enforced that He is extraordinary because no ordinary love
would do.
He helped me realize His love for me is real and true.
True to the fact that His love is from above,
A love sweeter than any ordinary love.

Once thinking I was a single, saved but unsatisfied woman.
Looking and searching and attempting to find all that I can.
Now, I have found the lover of my heart, my mind, my body and
my soul.
He is the man in whom I fully trust.
My life, to Him, I trust.
Now, I am a Single, Saved and Satisfied woman.

SOCIETY

That which has been is that which shall be; and that which has been done is that which shall be done: and there is no new thing under the sun.

ECCLESIASTES 1:9 (WEB)

THINK: WHAT'S NEXT

We could blame the parents and say they are not there,
We could break that down and say it's because they just don't care.
They'd rather be there and not here,
They'd show their love but with a closed ear.

THINK!

We could blame it on the school system and say they don't have a clue.
They hire uneducated educators,
That pretend to be true.
They don't allow raised voices nor raised hands.
They don't encourage students but push away the child's stance.

THINK!

We could blame it on society and say they are all about the money,
Walking around in their nice suits, driving their big cars and trying to get into the honey.
They vote against the good,
Yet say, "If only I could."
They lie, steal and cheat while saying, "For you, I would...."

THINK!

We could blame it on the government and say the little man don't count.
But they gather at big hotels, eat their big meals while keeping the average man out.
Yet they wonder why we don't trust them,
Nor believe what they say.
On that, I boldly stand and say

We are one!
Oh yes, we are one.

Your skin may be a different color than mine,
If you looked beneath the skin, you, too, will find,
The only difference between you and I is our spirit, soul and skin,
The true person is found heartfully within.

THINK!

We could blame the church and say they are busy hypocriting,
Sinning, losing souls, and whining.
Shining, fronting, but having a form of godliness.
At the same time, making a worldly mess.
Encouraging Santa Claus and the Easter Bunny,
But when it comes to Jesus Christ, they tend to act funny.

THINK!

We could blame it on the rain,
And say with rain comes pain.
Truth is things grow when it rains,
Without rain we'd endure much pain.
The sun would not shine,
Nor heat grapes into wine.
The ground would be dry.
Pollen count would be high.
Even the animals would ask why.

THINK!

Everything is now instant:
Microwaves, air fryers, tracks and gel nails,
Text messages, dm's and emails.
Instagram, Facebook and something called Twitter.
Less phone calls, no long walks, more time spent not together.
Date night now is maybe dinner but definitely sex.
People, oh people, I sadly ask, "What's next?"

THINK!

PRIORITIZE!!!

One of the greatest MISTAKES many of us make,
We sit in the back of the class,
Don't know what's first from what's last,
Can't for real read and are not trying to write,
And at birth, don't know our lefts from our rights.

But I can throw up one finger and say "SHHHHHH" or "F" that
brother.
Or two fingers up can say "PEACE" or "GOOD BYE" to a sister.
Three fingers to something is basically "OKAY"
Or quite frankly, some stuff I'm not permitted to say.
Four fingers can represent what side you live on.
Or to the deaf man, just "B."
Five fingers says "HI!"
Or Good Bye!
Or Talk to the Hand,
Cause I know you ain't talking to me.

One of the greatest MISTAKES that many of us make,
We sit in the back of the class,
Don't know what's first from what's last,
Can't for real read and are not trying to write,
At the age of five,
And don't know our lefts from our rights.

I can walk around as if life is all about me,
Neglecting the fact that the future is looking at me,
Trying to see who, what, when, where and why to be.
I try so hard to tell them to be who you are to be,
'Cause trying to be like me
They will lose who they are meant to be.

One of the greatest MISTAKES that many of us make,

We sit in the back of the class,
Don't know what's first from what's last,
Can't for real read and are not trying to write,
At the age of twenty-five,
And don't know our lefts from our rights.

But I can text "LOL!" "SMH!" or "ILY!"
As our babies stand reaching out crying,
"Mommy, hold me,"
"Daddy, show me,"
"Mommy, feed me,"
"Daddy, don't leave me,"
"I didn't ask to come here,
Why are you making me pay for your pleasure with my tears?"
"Please mommy,
I want you, not granny but you,"
"Come on daddy,
I want you, not uncle but you."

One of the greatest MISTAKES that many of us make,
We sit in the back of the class,
Don't know what's first from what's last,
Can't for real read and are not trying to write,
At the age of fifty- five,
And don't know our lefts from our rights.

Sports we watch,
Video games, we play,
Burgers we eat,
Codes we say,
Only physical activity we have is sex,
I pause to ask my people,
What's next?

One of the greatest MISTAKES that many of us make,
We sit in the back of the class,
Don't know what's first from what's last,
Can't for real read and are not trying to write,
At the point of death,
And still don't know our lefts from our rights.

PRIORITIZE!!!

THINGS GROW WHEN IT RAINS

As said in days of old, "When it rains, it pours."
Some look at rain as an eye-sore
As a hindrance to their flow,
As a damper of their day,
As a definite no-no,
As a slower of their way.

If there were no rain,
The land would endure much pain,
The ground would go dry,
The animals would die,
The grass would strain,
All Because there is no rain.

Fresh veggies we would not eat,
Sour fruits would never become sweet.
Elevated temperatures,
With more and more closed doors,
Less people coming out of the house
More folks running around like a mouse.
Ducking and diving simple liberties,
No visitors, no come throughs, no loving gatherings,
Around the grill,
As friends sit and chill,
And laugh as they talk,
And take long walks,
Not to go insane,
But none would be, because of no rain.

Yea, the sun would always shine
Heating grapes, as they become wine.
You dial number after number in search to find,
That loving someone you may never call mine.

All this because things have gone insane
Because there is no rain.

See, my dear, things surely do grow when it rains.
No, the sun won't always shine
Neither will you always endure pain.
Every so often you will cross peace!
Trouble will soon completely cease!
Life will go on and on and on
Until Jesus returns and the final trumpet is rung.
But until that time comes and all for real goes insane
Please remember
Things grow when it rains.

OUR PRESENT HISTORY

"Lift every voice and sing, 'til earth and Heaven ring,
Ring with the harmony of liberty."

Liberty, is that the true way to be,
Or just a state of being of how we are supposed to be?
Or is it the ability to reach back and pull another forward
And be who you are called to be?
Truth is, you being who you are Godly chosen to be
Makes life all worth the living.

"Let our rejoicing rise, high as the listening skies,
Let it resound, loud as the rolling sea."

See, back on January 01 of 1863,
The Emancipation Proclamation was signed
proclaiming to set us free.
Looking at things now and imagining how things were back then
I see things have changed, but not much
We are still bound in chains
And, it too, has not set us free.

We the people neglect to walk in the reality
Of the way threaded to set us free
Yet, we are choosing death
I say to give me liberty
'Cause I don't want what you have left.

"Sing a song full of the faith that the dark past has taught us.
Sing a song full of the hope that the present has brought us."

And is teaching us,
While rearing us,
To give us the flavor of us.
From our dark chocolate

To the off white and the many shades in between.
From our big hips to our luscious lips
From the curly hair to our firm voices that ring.

"Facing the rising sun of our new day begun,
Let us march on until victory is won."

But what is victory?
Is the battle already won or are we still fighting?

Am I trying to receive what belongs truly to me?
No matter how much I gather,
My battle is in the hustle
Amidst the chatter of wordless lips.
As we dodge the bullet or duck the knife,
While our sons and daughters endure misery and strife.
At school and at home,
At church and all alone,
The struggle is real.
For we cannot keep silent,
That is not a part of the deal.

United we stand, but we make divided decisions.
We say "I Love You",
But with closed ears we try to listen.
With empty hearts we multiply.
With selfish minds we subtract.
When reality sets in,
The woulda, shoulda, couldas
Come rolling back
To our minds,
As we drink or smoke to try to unwind.

Regardless of what's what,
I will always be considered black.
No matter how I straighten my hair
With the creamy crack.

Or stand strong with an arch in my back,
Which makes my chest rise,
As I lift my eyes towards the unfriendly skies,
I painfully yet boldly pray.

"Shadowed beneath Thy hand,
May we forever stand
True to our God and true to our native land."

"For out from a gloomy past,
'Til now we stand at last
Where the white gleam
Of our bright star is cast."

"So, facing the rising sun
Of our new day begun
Let us march on,
'Til victory is won."

REALITY

Reality, if you face it,
You too will see,
Just how life is supposed to be.

From a blizzard in the mid spring,
To severe hot temperatures in the fall,
To multiple tornadoes coast to coast,
Days and weeks of no rain at all.

From bold belittlement because of one's race,
To deliberate differences in one's pay rate,
To constant inconsiderate divisive decisions,
To violated voices hushed to sharing their suggestions.

Reality, if you face it,
You too will see,
Just how life is supposed to be.

Opportunities missed to opportunist's risk,
Another chance taken because you took a stand,
And shot your shot,
'Cause only you can stop
…..you.

Rise up my dear and do you,
Love on you.
Demand to be respected,
With no excuses accepted.
Step out and try your best,
Compare not thyself to the rest.
There is only one true you,
Let others always see you love you,
Due to how you love others,
Remember, we are all sisters and brothers.

Reality, if you face it,
You too will see,
Just how life is supposed to be.

Many misjudge the book by the cover,
Overlooking the best choice
Via the lies of others.
Please, ask me about me.
Only God and I really know me.
Only God and you really know you.
So, just keep it real in all you
Say, be, think and do.

The five senses can make you look like a fool.
Use your common sense as you go through life's school.
Once you graduate from school to school,
You always have a chance to learn.
A lesson can come from a child,
A rock, a dream, a song....
Pay closer attention when things start to go wrong.
Maybe it is time to take another step.
God said, If you trust Him, before you make a step,
He will be your next step's help.

Reality, if you face it,
You too, will see,
Just how life is supposed to be.

God knows His plans
Which outweighs your plans.
Not some of the world, but
The whole world is in His hands.

Nothing you encounter is a surprise, by chance.
Remember to consider others and their life's stance.
All things considered before you make a move,
For, every round goes higher and higher.
It is all up to the God in you,
To make the devil a liar.

Reality, if you face it,
You too will see,
Just how life is supposed to be.

TOMORROW'S HISTORY

Today is tomorrow's history.
Today's choice is a part of your life's story.
Today's decisions could be the major reason,
Tomorrow's weather could be a change in seasons.

Do I say I do because I'm getting old?
Do I do what I want because I am bold?
Do I think on the thoughts flowing concurrently with my day?
Do I agree with society around me or strike out and go my own
way?

Don't get left behind
Trying to mind
The flow and time
Of another's life's unwind,
Wasted time, one can never rewind.

Make use of today's time.
Waiting for tomorrow is an unnecessary crime,
Committed by plenty
Who had many,
A chance and opportunity
To rise up and see
How to step out and be,
More today in every way
As they jump today
And make good use of the day.

For it, too, is a part of your life's journey
As you pursue life
Living your story,
Don't be so quick to say yes or no
Because it makes you seem thirsty.

It's an awesome ability to push towards destiny
Living out the liberty
Set to show others the victory
You occurred today
By looking forward to tomorrow's history.

F AMILY

...As for me and my house, we will serve the Lord.

JOSHUA 24:15 PART B (KJV)

FAMILY

Hi, my name is.....

Hello, my name is .....

Excuse me, my name is..... Conflicted.

See, my father is Misguided

And my mother, she's Misused.

My sister is Confused.

My brother is Abused.

My aunt is Misunderstood.

My uncle is Misjudged.

My cousins are Ashamed

Because they are called Mister and Misconstrued.

I, Conflicted, don't know how to choose,

Much like my fore-father's, I too, am unguided and unused.

THE SOUNDS OF THE NIGHT

Have you ever noticed the radio is automatically louder at night?
Try it, you will see that it gets louder with the passing of the day.
Early in the morning many noises exist.
By lunch time things are well on their way.

From the horn honked at the one's late,
The school bus's chuckles as it waits,
To the zing of the toaster,
To the scramble of eggs,
To the slam of car doors,
To the rumble of the keys,
Or to the opening of the store's door.

To the neighbors saying their good mornings,
To the flop of the runner's shoes,
To the sigh of mom as she drops the kids off at school,
To the running of dad off to work, reading last night's news.

Oh, but as the day goes on and life progresses,
People tend to their moment by moment business.
The sounds of the day get more and more intense.
But as soon as night falls,
Things get less and less of an offense.
To the clutter of time,
So now, sit back and unwind,
And chill or just be,
As the sounds of the night softly increase.

Less yelling and selling and bargaining and bidding,
More enjoying and eating and chatting and chilling.
Which leads to more snoring and some deep breathing,
To tossing and turning and flipping and teasing.
Which all can lead to some much needed healing.

Followed by birds chirping, crickets twitching and a rooster
crowing.
Just some of the things in a day's process,
That's all about to start over,
With the dawn of a new day,
Goes away,
The sounds of the night.

LIFE

Life, a flow that comes and goes,
But few, few people really know
What it means to live their own life.

As a child, mom and dad says,
"One day you will be like me!"

But mom and dad is that really
How you want your child to be?

Are your steps really good to follow in
Or should you desire them to set their own trend?
Be who God created them to be
Because being like you,
They may miss who they are to truly be.

Being like you could be their fate.
Not saying that is a bad thing,
But some things are better found out as you wait.
The saying does say,
"Good things come to those who wait."
Many things are inevitable,
That you will see.
Just wait!

From conception to death,
Life is a constantly moving progress.
Even as you lay down to rest,
That too, is a part of the process.
At times you are at peace,
And other times you need stress to cease.
Regardless if you are two months
Or have two months of life left,
Make the most of the moment

And enjoy all of yourself.
Live each moment to the fullest,
Rise above it all to be your best,
Whether you have a Doctorate,
A Master's or a Bachelor's degree,
Or you only graduated from high school
Or somewhere below 12th grade you be.
Regardless of the accolades applied to your name,
It really does not matter,
In the end, we are all the same.
What you do with what you have makes the difference.
It is all in accordance with your life's preference.

If you have a house or an apartment,
Or you live in your parent's basement,
If you have two kids, ten kids or no kids,
If you are a virgin, a re-virgin or screwing out both pants legs,
If you make 10G's, 20G's or 100G's a year,
Or you don't have a job and live off your tears.

Regardless of the flow of your life,
Be sure to live your own life.
Do not inflict on other folks misery and strife,
Because you chose not to live your own life.

THESE ARE A FEW OF MY FAVORITE THINGS

The smile of a child when they succeed a goal.
The flow of a mother when her child she holds.
The determining factor of a manly man's drive.
The destination met because you have now arrived.

The smell of home after a long day's do.
The feel of my bed after I've done all I was supposed to do.
These too are a few of my favorite things.

The smell of my soap
As I soak in a sweet bubble bath.
The stomachache after a good hard laugh.
The smell of my boo after he walks out the door.
The sound of his morning voice as he hits the floor.

The aura of my parents as I enter their home.
The memories of my grannies as my mind looks back and roam.
These too are a few of my favorite things.

The shade of blue from the state trooper's lights but not behind me.
The taste of pineapples and cottage cheese as I allow it to please me.
The flavor of hazelnut creamer as it blends perfectly with my coffee.
The feel of my pen as I write what's within me.

The sound of music as I play a tune that resonates from me.
To chill with my best friend over a meal and a bottle of wine.
To watch the Golden Girls and laugh until I'm crying.
These too are a few of my favorite things.

The much needed hug when it is needed the most.

That unified thought neither of you are afraid to post.
That text message sent to simply say, "Hi!"
That pause because neither of you wants to be the first to say
goodbye.

That augmented chord over the diminished third.
The preacher's recap of what He, from God, heard.
The husband's kiss, the brother's support.
The child's reach out, the family's resort.
These too, are a few of my favorite things.

MY' DEA

I remember the sweet smile you always gave,
The from scratch cornbread you made us make.
How you fine cut your collard greens,
Shucked corn,
And snapped purple hulled peas.
How you lovingly attended everybody's kids,
Whooped us,
Yet loved us no matter what we did.

How you picked mangos and shared your plums,
How you sat on the porch and rocking was your fun.
I remember all the joys you brought to my life
And no matter the wrong,
You knew how to make us "get right"

Dea, with you I had:
      Comfort without cost,
      Peace when I was lost,
      Rest when I was tired,
      A job when I got fired,
      Covering, regardless of the storm,
      The beginning of my heart's reform,
      The place I could go to relax and be free,
      The one who knew the truest me,

There is absolutely NO PLACE LIKE HOME!
There Is NO PLACE LIKE HOME!!
THERE IS NO PLACE LIKE HOME!!!
It's there, I can dream a million dreams,
Have things be more than they seem,
Enjoy All In the Family, literally,
Get married, have babies and even die, happily.

It is there we gather, we eat, we sleep, we show,
We smile, we frown, we fuss, we grow.

We learned to cook.
We learned to clean.
We learned to be nice.
We learned to be nicely mean.
It is there we valued people, regardless of their skin.
We understood the strength of a real friend.
We vastly leave but can freely return,
We explored the world, experienced life and money earned.

Because of you, I want to be the best granddaughter I can be,
A number one sister I hope they will call me,
A true friend without fight or fallout,
A true committed wife, without waiver or doubt;
Taking care of home,
Sometimes all alone,
Doing whatever is needed to be done,
While to myself, remaining true.

Regardless of who's who or where life goes,
Always remember to make sure that everybody knows,
Whether they are two, twenty, fifty or one hundred years old,
There is NO PLACE LIKE HOME!
There Is NO PLACE LIKE HOME!!
THERE IS NO PLACE LIKE HOME!!!

L OVINGLY

Let all that you do be done in love.

I CORINTHIANS 16:14 (WEB)

SIGNS OF LOVE

It's that blue sky on a cloudy day,
That glimmer of sunshine on a rainy day,
That green light as traffic gets out of your way,
That joyful notion when you don't know what to say.

It's that calm and peace after the storm has gone,
That last note played after the song has been sung,
That first word spoken after a good night's rest,
That sigh of relief because you've done your best.

It's that vacuum cleaner instead of the broom,
That sign on the front door saying, opening soon,
That familiar chord played at the beginning of a song,
That organized chaos when all else is going wrong.

It's that having your umbrella along with your raincoat,
That pat on the back when you begin to choke,
That stop of the taxi; that raise on your job,
That sip of Red Bull when staying awake gets hard.

It's that longer than expected, yet much needed hug,
That electrical outlet when your phone needs a plug,
That two pack of Stanback when your head aches,
That plate of your momma's cooking when your belly and heart
aches.

It's that slice of red velvet cake with vanilla ice cream and a tall
glass of wine,
That sweet pair of Michael Kors shades in the summertime,
In Alabama, in the 99 degree sunshine.
That dinner invite from a friend,
Because they knew you were hungry and tired,
And did not want to cook,

That benediction from church,
'Cause you prefer the game be at what you look......
At, while your boo grill's,
And you and your bestie chill,
Or you hear the repeated words "Keep it real!"

It's that kiss sweetly given as you two say good night,
That instinct reminder that everything is already alright,
That email received saying your package has been shipped,
That pretty pair of pumps and purse perfectly picked.

It's that upgrade given just because you deserved it,
That front row concert seat precisely placed just like you re-
served it,
That morning's favored flavored frappe' properly mixed and
served,
That open highway with no police eye observed.

In case you haven't discovered what I'm talking about,
It's that heart's desire without hurt or doubt.

It's that simple, yet complex SIGN OF LOVE.

HEART-TEST

Among the heart-test things in this world,
Is to see your man with another girl.
Or your girl with another man.
Regardless of your stance,
It'll set your heart on quicksand.

Reality sets in with every moment and every thought,
As you see them walk,
Hand in hand.
Imagining their eye contact,
And subtle forehead kiss.

Oh, how you wish you didn't miss them anymore,
Or simply done things differently.

How you, minus one of them, could be
Fellows you and she,
Or Ladies you and he.
But right now, there can't be a loving we,
Because it's him and her or he and she.

But with every glance,
Your mind does a dance
While remembering and hoping, yet wishing
As you imagine them in your arms instead.
Smiling big amidst the heartless charm,
Still raining moment after moment with loving charm.

But the daydream can't last,
So mentally erase the past.
Move on,
'Cause they have already begun their next chapter,
So humbly replace the hurt, with an out loud laughter.

Maybe just maybe,
They will come back asking
For another opportunity,
To be
First in your heart.
Do you give in and start a new start
Or blissfully remember why you two are apart?

Don't you dare ask me for forever
Especially when you had me!
And I know, you know I'll NEVA TRUST thee,
With anymore of me,
'Cause I gave you the best of me.
Do you really think I would,
Allow you to have access to the rest of me?
So you could possibly,
Hurt me,
Or desert me,
Or leave me,
Standing lonely.

My heart nor my mind would permit me
To let thee ever back next to me.

At one point, all of me loved all of you.
All your bent curves, and your jagged edges,
Your imperfections
Your pettiness,
And dramatic mess.
Baby I realized,
Your brokenness with my wholeness,
Will sadly make a whole mess.
So I moved on,
As I should.

Please, follow not just your mind and trust with your heart,
Look with the Spirit from the very start.
'Cause the blinded move is like taking, an unstudied for test,
When you look and you realize, that this too was only a HEART-
TEST.

POSSIBLE PURPOSE

I remember the day I met you,
And your humble light did shine,
You greeted me with a smile,
Then everything else just fell in line.

From that day until this day,
I honestly can say,
You've driven my life crazy,
In every which way.

We've prayed together,
Worked together,
Ministered together,
Honored God together.

We've studied the Word together,
Fell on our knees together,
Traveled together,
Became friends together.

I bless the Lord for you,
And all He's placed in you.
You have propelled me towards purpose,
Awakened a newness,
Next to God and family, in line is you.
Sad to say, but I proudly say,
I think I'm addicted to you.

You're an angel, a godsend,
A true and dedicated friend.
I trust you unlike any other,
You stand with me, just like my brother.
I've got your back just like you've got mine.
I hope, as time goes, together our lights will shine

Through the good and the bad
The ups and the downs
The no-matter-what's
I promise to always be around.

If you could, I believe you would give me the world,
And all that I prefer.
I believe you would stand with me,
Across every river
Unlike just any average friend.
You give smiles when I am down,
Lots of love when I am alone,
A life raft before I drown,
That text to make sure I made it home.

Distance is what is between us,
But even that is for us,
Determination minus frustration,
Leads to that united destination.

A WOMAN SCARRED

Broken and battered
But beautifully built.
Head and hands held harmoniously high,
Because my knees I've humbly knelt.
Heart's been shattered,
The pieces so many I could not gather.
Too scattered to see,
How to get my heart to love correctly.

From my dad:
That first humbling hug and kindled forehead kiss,
That first cozy cuddle
An unasked wish
…. granted.
As the twinkle in my eyes to his eyes
Enchanted,
Entangled,
Mingled and managed.
To his baby girl chanted
To be her protector
Her provider, her personal sacrifice,
Her example of a real man,
The best man ever in her life.
He called me baby girl and I called him Dr. Dad.
He has shown to be the hardest, truest guy
My life has ever had.

From my best guy friend:
He taught me how to never trust the he
But to watch the he
That tries to get next to me.
Listen to the words he does not say,

Pay close attention to what he does during the day,
It is hard to see what is shown at night.
Be mindful of the he that only does you *his* version of right.
When you are out of plain sight,
As he pretends to love you,
Yet really keeps you out of the light
As with his eyes, he too, fight
To not see you standing bright.
Then you remember your friend said to keep it real.
'Cause loving on and not loving
Was the real deal.

From the lover of me:
The lover of the night
Which never, ever felt right
No matter how strong the hold
Only my body could he hold.
It was never my body, soul, heart and mind,
The total me he never took time to find.

Broken and battered,
But beautifully built.
Head and hands held harmoniously high,
Because my knees I've humbly knelt.
Heart's been shattered,
The pieces so many I could not gather.
Too scattered to see,
How to get my heart to loving correctly.

TRUST

Trust and believe
It's hard to conceive,
To push your mind to relieve,
The honest notion your love they received.
It's not always easy
Once trust has been broken,
To let another in
To possibly mistreat your love token.

Trust
As you take a chance
To protect you stance,
Yet miss your next heart's dance.
Broken and battered, hurt and abused
Left going in circles, left confused,
Not knowing what direction you are to choose,
Too afraid you will lose
Another beat of your heart's blues.

Trust and go
With life's flow
From birth to death.
And all that is in between
Learn to lean
Not on how you want it to be,
But trust God
And seek God
And believe God

As He directs you through
What He has planned for you.

Trust and see
It won't always be easy
But run on and see
Just how the ends gonna be
You just might experience
What is really best for thee,
As you rise up and fly free
Trusting and living life abundantly.

Trust and do
As you are supposed to do
Always to thine own self be true
Promise not to lie
So rise up and try
Give your best
If anything is left
Don't keep it for yourself
For love is as love does
Push through with love
It will push you to push
Another to rise above.

WHAT IT REALLY MEANS TO LOVE!?

Love!?

Is it the touch of a hand
Or the grace of your stand
Or the joy of a voice
Or the options of making a choice

Love!?

Is it the sweet smell after the rain
Or the assurance of peace during the pain
Or the money made after a workday
Or the grade made after you wrote an essay

Love!?

Love is patient and kind
It is sweet and don't mind
Standing with you in all you do
It lets you be you
And me be me

Love!?

Love is understanding and caring
It is sharing and declaring
Decreeing and being, bringing and giving
Loving and living, doing and seeing
Touching and hearing, forgiving and supporting
Providing and protecting

Love!?

It is never neglecting nor misleading
Deceiving nor unbelieving
It is always abundant, an assurance, a life bringing guarantee
Better than a life insurance policy

Love!?

It is that peace of mind
That helps you unwind,
That wants to always be kind
That drive out the way
In order to find

It is that hot bowl of chicken noodle soup
That makes you jump through hoops
Or run mile after mile
Or jump loop to loop

Love!?

Is it that late night text
Or that pause to see what's next
Or that early morning kiss
You know, that call just as
You start to miss....

Their presence, their smile
Their smell, their hug
Their snore, their silence
You know, that...all of them.

It's all in that experience called LOVE!?

JUST LIKE THAT.....

I want an Adam and Eve kind of love,
...that Claire and Cliff Huxtable kind of love,
...that Romeo and Juliette kind of love,
...that Barak and Michelle kind of love,
You know, that Will and Jada kind of love.

That love that makes you compete kind of love.
That over the river and through the woods,
Passed grandma house, to the backyard kind of love.
You know, that kind of love that says we are going to stand the test of time,
As we let our lives together unwind, kind of love.

I want that kind of love where he wakes in the middle of the night
And don't feel me
As he's not yet realized I might have just gone to see......
As he runs through the house looking for me,
I raise my voice to say, "Hey babe, I'm in the bathroom
I ain't going nowhere."......kind of love.

I want that kind of love that says, "I love you, you love me
Let's make the next best family."

I want that kind of love that says, "With you, baby, I will always be....true."
For better or worse, richer or poorer,
In sickness and in health,
Forsaking all others, for as long as we both shall live, kind of love.

So to you I give all of me
'Cause all of me loves every single bit of you,
Your curves and your nerves
Your you-ness, your uniqueness.

I love everything about you.
From the snore of you
To the smell of you
To the way you hold me
And console me
To how I even let you semi-control me.

I give God all of me and I want a man that gives God all of he.
All I get is God's leftovers.
That is enough for me!

I want a love JUST LIKE THAT!!!

NIGHT DAYDREAMING

Deep in thought as you look around to try to see,
And grasp the many scenes shown before thee.
From the happenings of the time past,
To the want of another, just like the other night's last…

…glass of wine.
As your mind starts to drift,
You start to picturing and imagining
As your thoughts begin to lift
You higher and higher
Then with every turn
As your heart yearns
To see what is to come.

An enchantment accessed only by some
'Cause not every one's enabled to come
And see how the end is going to be,

For thee and sometimes we,
As your thoughts become the scene you see,
Play out step by step before me,
But only me can somehow see
The thoughts I have displayed before me.

As my thoughts roam farther,
Which makes it harder to walk away,
'Cause I want to know which way
The dream will come about,
This thought ain't no ordinary thought, no doubt.
I try my best to move on
And see how it will play out.

…At least in my head,

You would think I am in my bed,
But I feel the night's air breeze,
Which helps me to deeper breathe,
Which helps me to deeper see,
Which helps my thoughts to deeper be,
Deeper in peace,
In a deep place,
Where I can't see your face, but I know it's you,
'Cause of how you do what you do.

Just as you were about to be ....
I was awakened by the touch of real reality.

GOD SAVED ME

Jesus said to him, "I am the way, the truth, and the life. No one comes to the Father, except through me."

JOHN 14:6 (WEB)

IF IT HAD NOT BEEN

Let the people say,
If it had not been for the Lord on my side
I ain't even gotta tell you where I'd be
'Cause standing before you today
That option would not be.

Not only did He keep our enemies away,
He allowed us to see a brand new day.
Again and again and again and again
He's blessed us and kept us,
Which is His hand's constant trend.

He gives each day, our daily bread
He's so good we can even live by what He said.
My house may not be as big as yours,
But we both have a home.
You may have 20 friends and I only 2
But regardless He promised to never leave us alone.

He asks us to trust Him
With all of who we are,
And He will direct our steps.
That says to me
Every single bit of me,
He's kept me,
All along the way.
Guiding me, directing me
Even giving me the words I am to say.

Whether you have lived the promised three score and ten years,
Or you've passed that number, headed to those glorious years,
Or you have only made it to but a fraction of that,
We all can stand on that awesome fact,

Just as King David said, as He too, looked back,
If it had not been for the Lord on my side
Can everybody, somebody, please anybody tell me where would
we be?
I, too, want to know where you would be?

As I look back
And graciously think back
I too, can say,
There have been some good days,

And some days the sun didn't quite shine,
In all honesty, as I look around and reality begins to unwind
The sun shining days outnumber the rainy days
I smile, because again, God has made another way.

God has been, is and will always be good
We must trust Him as we should.

Smile as you now declare and decree, personally,
If it had not been for the Lord on my side
In hell is where I'd already be.

You don't have to answer me,
Because I've already told me,
If it had not been for the Lord on my side,
I undoubtedly know where I would be.

SPEAK TO ME!!!

I OPENED THE EYES OF MY HEART AND I WON'T TURN BACK.
I'M LOOKING! I'M LISTENING! I'M SEEKING ONLY FOR THE FACT
OF THE MATTER IS, KNOW WHAT THE MATTER IS . . . .
WHETHER IT IS THAT . . . . OR WHETHER IT IS THIS . . . . .

SPEAK LORD, SPEAK TO ME!!!

I OPENED THE EYES OF MY MIND
ON THE SEARCH TO FIND
THAT LOVE, THAT WILL STAND
THE TEST OF TIME
ONLY TO COME TO KNOW THAT LOVE IS AS LOVE DOES. . . .
NO LIMITS, NO BOUNDARIES, NO BUTS, NO BECAUSE. . . . .

SPEAK LORD, SPEAK TO ME!!!

I OPENED THE EYES OF MY BODY,
YET I CLOSED THE SPIRITUAL ME,
BUT THE MORE I HELD ON,
THE FARTHER I GOT FROM WHAT WAS WITHIN
ME.
NO LOVE, I FOUND! NOT LOVE BY MY DEFINE!
NOW I SIT ALONE, WITH AN OPEN BODY, CRYING!

SPEAK LORD, SPEAK TO ME!!!

I OPENED THE EYES OF MY SOUL,
ONLY TO OUR LORD AND SAVIOR.
MY SOUL HE HOLDS.
SORRY DEMON, FOR TRYING TO GET AT ME.
THE STANDARD HAS BEEN LIFTED.
DON'T WASTE YOUR TIME,
CAUSE UNDER GOD'S WING IS WHERE I'LL BE.

SPEAK LORD, SPEAK TO ME!!!

SPEAK LORD, SPEAK TO ME!
SPEAK LORD, SPEAK TO ME!!
SPEAK LORD, SPEAK TO ME!!!
MY HEART, MY MIND, MY BODY AND MY SOUL, TO YOU ARE OPENED.
SPEAK LORD, SPEAK TO ME!!!

DELIVER ME

Lord please!
Dear Father God please
Deliver me,
From that which hinders me
From being all that you created me
To wake up, get up, make my bed up and be
For I'm trying, Lord,
To kill the made me
That life has dealt me
The decision maker's hand to apologetically be.

Regardless of what is going on
Or happening, standing blocking,
While trying to stop thee
From doing that one thing
To bring you to that perfected place of peace
Where all troubles cease
And chose to live and not lie as deceased,
'Cause I've made my mind up to be at ease
Not to wobble in that which was not meant to be
Because of the doctor's, lawyer's or whomever's report I choose
to believe.

Lord please!
Dear Father God please
Deliver me,
From that which hinders me
From being all that you created me
To wake up, get up, make my bed up and be
For I'm trying, Lord,
To kill the made me
That life has dealt me

The decision maker's hand to apologetically be.

So I stop selling myself short
Of whom I am to bring forth
So I leave that behind
While the true me, I now seek the Lord to find
Lord, please deliver me,
'Cause all I seem to do is hurt the me
And desert the me
While neglecting the me
You planned me to fully be.

Lord, I have cried my last broken hearted tear
Been silent the last time out of rejection and fear
Went left the last time because I chose not to hear
Had my last missed opportunity because I neglected to be here
Or where….. Ever I needed to be
To show off the true me,
The real me ,You created me to be.

Lord please!
Dear Father God please
Deliver me,
From that which hinders me
From being all that you created me
To wake up, get up, make my bed up and be
For I'm trying, Lord, to kill the made me
That life has dealt me
The decision maker's hand to apologetically be.

Whether it is a dessert decision of what food I shouldn't have ate,
What direction to go, although I am running a little late,
What college to attend, even though they actually chose me,
What movie to watch, although I know what I came to see,
Whether I say yes to the dress
Or close my ears to some mess
Or simply say not yet

'Cause I am supposed to wait
On God to guide me
To His planned escape
Which is His planned fate.
So no matter what
I hold fast to the profession of my faith
As I stand humble
Down on my knees I go
I loudly say
Lord please!
Dear Father God please
Deliver me,
From that which hinders me
From being all that you created me
To wake up, get up, make my bed up and be
For I'm trying, Lord, to kill the made me
That life has dealt me
The decision maker's hand to apologetically be.

"I DO"

Many have said, "My life, really, is not my own,
To the Lord I am supposed to belong."
But did we really mean it?
If God asked you for your heart
Would you give it?
If He asked for your child
Would you submit it?
If He asked you for your time
Would you subject it?
If He asked you for your all,
Would you surrender it?

We sing "I surrender all,"
But to ourselves we tend to fall
Victim to the world, the flesh and the devil.
Our life's three enemies
While we struggle with the inner me
While trying to be who we are supposed to be,
 All while resisting the enemy
As we try to be who God created us to be,

So, my life, I DO give
My love, I DO give
My all, I DO too give

I do!

Yes, I am the woman that said,
"Dear Lord, I do!"
For better or worse,
I do!
For richer or poorer,

I do!
Forsaking all others,
Lord, I do!

Lord,
I can't live,
If living is without you.
I can't love,
If loving is not like you.

I give my heart and my mind,
My body and my soul,
I give you my spirit,
Because it too,
You hold.

I give You all of my living,
It is in You that I move,
In You I exist,
And I have my being.

So my life, I DO give.
My love, I DO give.
My all, I DO too give.

I AM GOD

God said to tell you,
"I AM GOD".
Why is it that you make your own life so hard?
By seeking the he or she that also has to see Me.
When trusting Me and obeying Me
Is what you need to do, to be.
Before it all began,
I Am, was there.
Through it all, I Am the He who really cares.
When it is all said and done
I have already told you and showed you,
The victory, I've already won.

You refuse to seek Me,
But I planned every day.
You refused to stand,
But you can stand on every word I say,
If I said you were healed,
You were healed.
If I said it, It is so,
You just keep it real.
If I said don't worry,
Trust and believe, I've got your back.
If I said put a period.
It is an absolute fact.

If I said I will make a way,
No matter how high the hill,
Low the valley or big the giant,
I have made a way.
Whether I allow you to see the plan
Or give you step by step,

Always know I AM your ever present help.

Regardless the ache, how large the lack,
If the Bible says it, it is still a fact.
Those are your Basic Instructions, Before Leaving Earth.
I had your life planned, before your mother gave birth.

So okay, please don't get it twisted,
God is God, with or without you
He is strong, so of course, He will do whatever He plans to do.
You need Him.
Aahhh without Him,
We are all lost.
Each and every one of us, it is true.

God is Alpha and Omega,
The first and the last.
Whatever you need,
I dare you, to sincerely ask.

God is a friend to the friendless,
Hope for the hopeless,
A belt when you need a whooping,
A rod when you need correcting.
He is strong when your body is weak.
He is a strong hand, when your mind is weak.
He is that interception, when your team's about to lose.
He is that intercession, when hell is your soul's blues.

Think you are invincible,
Die and you will be replaced.
The enemy is on the rise,
God will feed you in their face.
Back is up against the wall,
A standard He will lift.
If push comes to shove,
Even time, He can shift.

God said,

> I Am the first and the last
> Whatever you need
> I dare you to just ask
> For I AM
>> I AM
>> I AM GOD.

THE RE-TURN

God's Son is coming back,
But only God knows when,
I behoove you to be ready
My brothers, my sisters,
My neighbors and my friends.

Instead of chilling and thinking,
Hoping time is on your side.
If you are not ready,
You will be left behind.

Times is not as long as it has been,
Sickness, homicide, suicide all self-centered sin.
So you better wake up, repent and realize,
Before in hell, you lift up your eyes.

ABOUT THE AUTHOR

Tabatha J. Jones

"With man this is impossible; but with God, all things are possible (Matthew 19:26)."

Let's talk about Tabatha "Joy" Jones! Born in 1978, in Greensboro, Alabama.
Tabatha Joy Jones was a bundle of "JOY" then, just as she is now.

The name Joy represents everything its meaning implies. She is assigned to be a means of delight, happiness and enjoyment, at all times, to all people, places and situations.

Tabatha adamantly believes in letting her little light shine.

She is an educated musician and has a Bachelor of Arts degree in Music Performance, and is a graduate of Judson College in Marion, Alabama.

Along with being a Minister of Music, she serves our Father by teacher and preaching His Holy Word.

Professionally Tabatha teaches music lessons for King Roper School of Music. She offers private lessons as well.